Inspirations

Tammy Flewelling

 HATCHBACK Publishing
Genesee, Michigan

Tammy's Timeless Inspirations
©2015 Tammy Flewelling

HATCHBACK Publishing, LLC.
P.O. Box 494
Genesee, Michigan 48437
Since 2005
www.chatcherenterprises.com

The views, opinions and words expressed in this book are those of the author and do not necessarily reflect the position of HATCHBACK Publishing LLC or its owners.

Library of Congress Control Number
2015937069

ISBN: 978-0-9891934-4-3

10 9 8 7 6 5 4 3 2 1

First Edition

Printed in the United States of America

For Worldwide Distribution

Contents

Introduction

This is a small collection of feelings I've put into words. This, I consider my therapy. Life can be trying at times. Putting pictures with my words enhances my visions of life. Hopefully others can relate to the words I've put on paper. I feel if I can connect with one person, then I have made a difference!

Having a vision is but a start. Acting on that vision makes it a reality. Let your inner self go, then like a river your feelings will flow. At this time your creation will fall into place, leaving you fulfilled, eventually filling that empty space.

Acknowledgments

Thanks to everyone who helped me achieve this goal.
My daughter Holly, my biggest joy and inspiration. My husband Russ, for being patient and for the title he gave my book. My stepdaughter Kristi, for her computer skills and all her help, I couldn't have done this without her!
Diane Dudley from Hemlock, MI, thanks for your photography skills and constant friend-ship. Bob from Bob's Karat House in Saginaw, MI, you are a good friend who gently nudged me in the right direction and told me "God gave you talent and shame on you for not pursuing it."
Thanks to all the moms in my life, Judy W. for loving me unconditionally through all the good and bad. Judy K. for always putting my life into perspective. Jane U.D. for shaping me into the person I am today. Lorna S. for being my rock and supporting me through the many hard phases of my life.
My niece, Areanna Pulaski for designing the cover. Reid Calcott DDS from Saginaw, MI for being my biggest fan and buying my art. My good friends Debbie, Robin, Sue and Janice, without my friends my life would be empty. You all give me the faith I need, the love and support I crave and the encouragement to keep going.
Family is important, I love you all.

A Beautiful Sight

I am beautiful and take pride in showing you

that I have no bad side.

So as I pose for the camera,

a beautiful creature with many amazing features.

This moment the attention I will seize,

with my ponytail gently blowing in the breeze.

So take a good look before I take flight,

God made me for you to look at,

an amazing and beautiful sight.

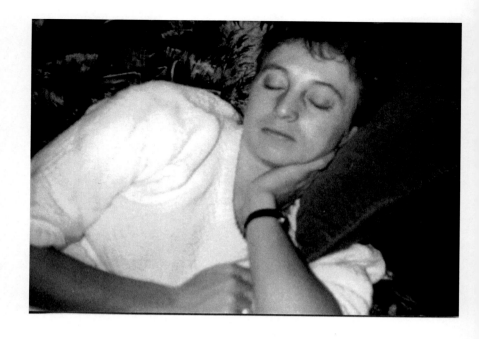

A Dream

Without a dream where would you be? We need a dream to paint a pretty picture of all the things we wish to see.

Without a dream there is only today, we need a dream to find our way.

Without a dream our hearts are empty, happy thoughts have no entry.

Without a dream our imaginations can't grow, a dream is like a garden we need to sow.

Without a dream, our feet remain rooted to one spot, with a dream we travel to places we'd thought we forgot.

Without a dream would we ever smile or would we see life as an endless trial?

We need a dream to envision what tomorrows can be used for, a dream is but a way to open many doors.

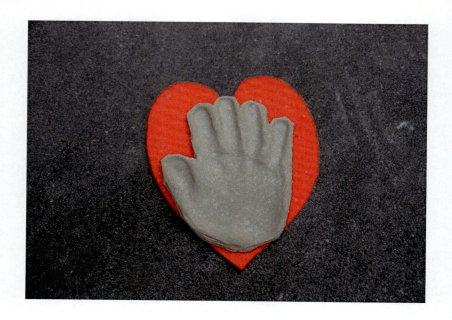

A Friend's Mark

A friend leaves a mark in our hearts
that time can't erase.

It's like a handprint dipped in cement.

It's everlasting, never fading.

It embraces our hearts from time to time.

A friend's mark will last forever, and will withstand
the test of time.

So if you have a friend's mark in your heart, you should count it as
one of your many blessings in life.

A Fine Wine

Share a glass of wine

with an old friend

Savoring a fine wine

and a timeless friendship

Both aged to perfection

A Lost Love

Regrets wash over me like a storm cloud threatening rain. I am not dealing well, with all of this pain!

Leaving you was wrong in so many ways, what if I had stayed? Would we be together today?

It's true when you lose something you only end up wanting it more, unfortunately, I was the one to close the door.

God help me, I think of you often, you may be out of sight, but not forgotten.

I'll never forgive myself for being so cruel. It's left me feeling like such a fool.

If only I had realized where I needed to be, then I wouldn't be here regretting not have a life without a you and a me.

A Rainbow

A rainbow promises a new day.

A day of endless sunshine.

A day of great possibilities.

A day to escape reality.

A day to go ahead and follow your rainbow,

A day to find your pot of gold.

My Best Friend

He's watched me try, he's watched me cry.

He's been my best friend, even when I'm at my wits end.

He's always right there by my side, as I go through life's crazy ride.

He makes life bearable when all else fails, he just looks at me and faithfully wags his tail.

I couldn't ask for anything more, a constant companion at my door.

A Second Chance

What if you woke up and realized the fog had lifted and you see things clearly for the first time in ages?

Would you then start a new chapter?
Would you turn to a new page?

Would you be given a second chance, due to all your past circumstances?

Would you be able to begin again, or at least be friends?
Would the bonds you've shared intervene, and fate could make you whole again?

Would the past become your present, or does it hold too much resentment?

What if a second chance was meant to be?
Is it something you could foresee?

What if hearts that have turned to stone, reunite and become one?

A second chance may be wishful thinking, but it just may come along.

So as the fog is lifting, you now may have the chance to dance, to a new and an old song.

A Wise Soul

A wise soul once told me to just let it go! To be angry all
the time just hurts you, not the ones you are angry at.

A wise soul once told me, always move forward, by looking
back you only stumble.
It's the steps forward that count, not the ones that caused you to
fall.

A wise soul once told me to find happiness within ourselves. To
think that money and material things are what we need for
happiness is only the failure to realize the true meaning of
happiness.

A wise soul once told me to forgive myself. Don't burden yourself
with what you've done wrong. You can't fix it, but you can learn
from it and move on.

A wise soul once told me to love what you have, and who you
are with. Take a good look at what you have and who you are
with, it's obviously where you belong or you wouldn't be there.

A wise soul once told me to never expect life to be easy,
learn to accept it and figure out how to deal with it. You
can't always control every situation or the outcome, so just
do the best you can, it's all that's expected of you.

A wise soul once told me, be grateful for what you have, less is more. If you think you are bad off take a good look around you, someone is always worse off than you.

A wise soul once told me, listen to your head, but lead with your heart. Your heart may sometimes steer you wrong from time to time, but without heart nothing has meaning.

Many wise souls have lived life to the fullest, loved with all their hearts, and learned a lot to pass on to others.

All I Want For You …

I want you to spread your wings and fly, never be afraid to try.

I want you to be comfortable in your own skin, not everyone's admiration you will win.

I want for you to always be true to yourself, this will be your ticket to happiness and wealth.

I want for you to never give up on your dreams, from your dreams, your inspiration will stream.

I want you to live life to the fullest, be an adventurer but yet a dreamer.

I want for you all the love in the world, for you are my one and only baby girl.

An Angel

Who knew I'd be sent an angel, to whom all my stories I could tell.

You blew me away by your insights and caring ways. You had a way of chasing all my fears and demons away.

Your kind words and gentle touch, will be for-ever present in my mind. I'd never met anyone like you, an angel that truly was a great find.

I am forever grateful for you reaching out to me. You saw in me what no one else could see.

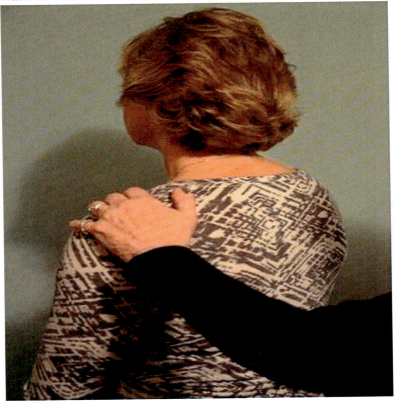

Another Day in Paradise

As we look at the pond glistening in the sun,
we are grateful for a place to congregate and have fun.

The hours we worked to make it picturesque,
were grueling, but worth it nevertheless.

Many memories have been made at our little paradise.
A special day was the day, we became husband and wife.

Our wedding was a picture perfect day,
and then we knew all the hard work we had endured,
was but a small sacrifice for
JUST ANOTHER DAY IN PARADISE!

Daughters

A daughter's love is a mere test of time,
dealing with attitudes that change on a dime.

You wouldn't trade them for anything, just treasure the days
they are happy and want to sing.

God made daughters to truly test our patience,
so keep this in mind when nothing else makes sense.

Just smile and realize, it won't always be this way.
After all, they will grow up someday!

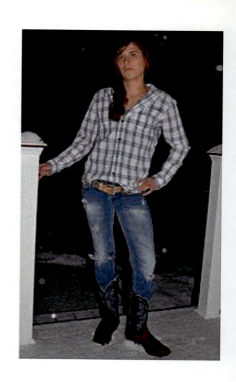

Baby Girl

I love you to the moon and back, it's your love that keeps me on track. Many mistakes I've made but you're not one, from your love I'll never run.

(chorus)
Baby girl you got to reach for the stars, after all they're not that far. Remember life is not as it seems. So baby hold tight to your many dreams.

It's a tough world baby watch your back, and don't worry about what you think you lack. God only knows it's an uphill climb, you'll get there, it just takes time.

Baby girl you got to reach for the stars, after all they're not that far. Remember life is not as it seems. So baby hold tight to your many dreams.

Baby you need to always take a chance and dance that dance. Life is your dance floor so twirl around. May your worries disappear and your answers be found.

Baby girl you got to reach for the stars, After all they're not that far. Remember life is not as it seems. So baby hold tight to your many dreams.

You've got to give each day a running start. Life will roll when you do your part. You just wait and see, the best days of your life are yet to be.

Baby girl you got to reach for the stars, after all they're not that far. Remember life is not as it seems, so baby hold tight to your many dreams.

Baby reach, reach really far and maybe someday you'll catch that falling star!

Be Inspired

Have you ever wondered about a path not taken?

A love not loved,

a gift not given,

a letter not written?

If only a chance to have your soul awakened,

to love and feel like you've met the perfect mate.

To give that gift that might have changed someone's world.

To write that letter that might have saved a friendship.

It's never too late to do something that might make a difference.

Take that path and see what lies ahead.

It could just be the perfect path to tread.

Happy Trails!

Just a Dream

I dreamt I was a turtle
I was named after my Grandma Myrtle
I was tough in my old shell
No worries, no fears, only happy stories to tell
I could be my laid back self
Sunshine, water, and adventures with friends
is what I considered my wealth
Well, I guess it's time to wake up from this dream
After all, life is never as it seems

Did You Ever Wonder…

Did you ever wake up and wonder, how did I get here?

What was I thinking or for that matter, drinking?

How could I do things I did or say the things I said?!

So many questions, so few answers,
so often a wall flower and not a dancer.

So many regrets of days gone by.
So many times, we hear ourselves say WHY?

Life is so complicated and surreal. When did we lose sight of what,
when, and how to feel?

We just need to face it, life is one messed up function that fails to
come with a list of instructions.

Just Maybe...

Just maybe our life's not based on faith but is based on our capability to hope.

Hoping some big or small act of kindness will be noticed and then our life will have purpose.

Just maybe faith is not about believing but is about hoping.

Hoping the truth will set us free and in our heart of hearts, love will conquer all.

So maybe hope is all we need.

Like a candle flickering in the dark, we hope it stays lit to guide us home.

Just maybe hope will see us through, with so many bad things going on in life. Maybe hope will let us find the good things life has to offer.

Just maybe life is based on hope?!

With hope we can face tomorrow, without hope there's only today.

So hope for the best and prepare for the worst.

Just maybe hope is all we need!

Life's Missing Pieces

Life is like a puzzle, we spend our time searching for the missing pieces.

Pieces that will determine our fate, and will lead us down the right path.

Pieces that will fill our hearts with joy and contentment.

Pieces that help restore our faith in others and ourselves.

Pieces that open new doors and close the ones that hold too many regrets.

Pieces like our hearts that are scattered all around.

Pieces that only we can configure back into place.

Go ahead and fill in the pieces to your puzzle, then and only then, you and your puzzle will be complete.

Life's Track

Sometimes life gets off track...

Your train has derailed leaving you trapped, with nowhere to go.

Life is funny that way, causing us to lose our bearings.
Like a fish in foreign water, going in circles lost and confused.

There is no estimate on time,
so your train could remain off track, unless you get a grip on
reality and focus on repairing the damage.

It won't be easy, it'll be the hardest thing you've ever done but
by fixing your track you can move on
and maybe your train will take you to the place you're meant to be.

Have Faith...

Life will always try to break you and repairs are often needed but
hold your head up high and face the track of life.

Loves Promise

Love promises to protect us from harm.
Love promises to be our lucky charm.

Love promises to never leave us alone.
Love promises to always be ours to own.

Love promises us happy ever after.
Love promises us days filled with laughter.

Love promises our cups will always be full.
Love promises to never be forgetful.

Love can promise us the moon.
Unfortunately, love is a promise that, sometimes ends too soon.

Memories

Some memories come to mind as easy as can be. The memories
that hurt too much we turn a blind eye and don't want to see.

For years we block out the memories that cause too much pain,
remembering them we feel we have nothing to gain.

Some memories we keep buried deep,
for if we let them surface, into our subconscious they will seep.

We try to remember important things from our past, sometimes
they come to mind briefly fleeing way too fast.

Some memories are meant to be kept at bay, except for the special
memories made from today.

My Daughter

I love you more than life itself. Your happiness to me is what I consider my wealth.

You know me better than anyone, thoughts of you bring me home again.

You've shared my hopes, my dreams and fears and God knows, many tears!

You're the best gift I've ever been given, you're my reason for living.

We share a bond like no other, the special bond between a daughter and a mother.

Pretty Girl

Hey pretty girl hold your head up high,
tomorrow's a new day with sunny skies.

It's really rough right now but it'll get better soon,
just have faith and shoot for the moon.

You have what it takes to make it in this tough world of ours,
so let your spirits soar.

Just remember the sky is the limit and you are the shining star in it.

The Mind

The mind is a powerful thing, it is in charge of everything.

Sometimes it means a sleepless night, tossing and turning trying to figure out how to make many wrongs right.

A mind can travel down many roads, often carrying too heavy a load.

A mind can keep us from seeing what is real, instead we are blinded by the hurt we feel.

A mind can be over loaded with doubt, too often leading us down the wrong route.

A mind could use some well deserved rest, for tomorrow's another day our minds will be put to the test.

The Past

The past looms over me like an ominous cloud filled with rain.
A past with too many wrongs and a lot of pain.

I hold it all in and hope my cloud doesn't burst, I always tend to
think the worst.

If only to go back and undo all the things I did to hurt the ones I
love. I'd send my cloud packing on the wings of a dove.

My cloud is getting bigger, darkness threatens to overtake me.
I want to return to the sunlight, a safe place to be.

I see the sun peaking out from under my dark cloud.
The sun is smiling she looks so proud.

Suddenly my spirits begin to soar.
Yeah, my dark cloud is gone and I feel like I have won this war!

Don't ever let the past dictate your life, just push past the bad and
think positive instead!

There's Something About the Water...

The sound, a pleasant song in your ears

The mist, a refreshing shower to your face

The beauty that lies before you,

A pleasant picture for your eyes

as your feet sink into the sand

You feel calm and relaxed

Take it all in and realize

there's just something about the water

True Friends

Life has dealt us some crappy cards

and on more than one occasion, we've been forced to fold.

As we are dealt another hand,

we know we have our friendship, on which we can hold.

The cards have been stacked against us,

more times than we care to remember.

Yet we know hearts are lucky,

and ours, no matter near or far, will always remain together.

So as the cards get shuffled once again,

we are confident the cards are in our favor,

and we will have a lasting friendship,

on which we can always depend.

Let the cards fall where they may,

because ours is a friendship that no card game can sway!

Walk Away

Walk away, walk away from feelings of betrayal.
Walk away, walk away from promises you can't keep.
Walk away, walk away from love gone wrong.

Walk into the sun, let it all go, feel happy, feel light, walk away
until it feels right.

Walk away, walk away from the over-whelmed feelings you can't
shake.
Walk away, walk away from feeling out of sorts with yourself.
Walk away, walk away from the disappointments, you've endured.

Walk into the sun, let it all go, feel happy, feel light, walk away
until it feels right.

Walk away, walk away from those who want to much from you.
Walk away, walk away from the things you can't change.
Walk away, walk away from someone's love and admiration you'll
never win.

Walk into the sun, let it all go, feel happy, feel light walk away
until it feels right.

Walk away, walk away from all the hurt yet to come.
Walk away, walk away, maybe it won't always be this way.
Walk away, walk away until your road has finally brought you
home.

When You Left

When you left I hurt so bad inside,
my feelings were raw I could not hide.

I just couldn't wrap my head around what went wrong.
My life had become a sad country song.

I walked through my days feeling alone and angry.
I just couldn't understand why you wanted to be free.

I of course blamed myself for holding on too tight.
I just couldn't see what was in plain sight.

I was having a hard time surfacing from all the hurt, my head felt
clouded and muddled with dirt.

I wasn't sure I could survive a betrayal like this.
I thought I had found that special someone to spend my life with.

The truth would soon rear its ugly head.
My heart would soon grow heavy and fill with dread.

I was never destined to be in your life, because you already had a
wife.

It was obvious I had made a huge mistake, from this nightmare I
needed to wake.

My heart was severally broken, and needed to heal, happiness
seemed so far away and surreal.

It's time to pick up the pieces of my broken heart, tomorrow's a
new day, a fresh start.

When You're Sad…

When you're feeling overwhelmed and sad,
may your heart grow wings and fly high above the clouds and sing.

Happy sounds will fill the air and then you'll realize,
what you need to get from here to there.

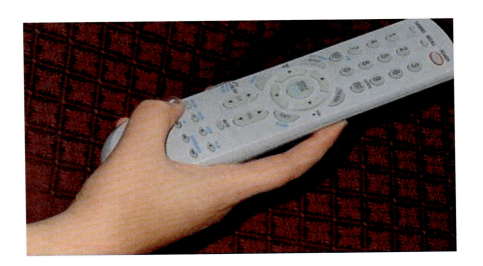

You Can't Go Back

Sometimes we care way too much, we
make decisions that time can't touch.

If only we could go back and push a
button and rewind.

Would it matter to have walked away?
Or does it matter anyway?

We can't undo or go back
but emotion we now lack.

It doesn't mean we don't care but to
reach out again, we don't dare.

Our love will remain the same, that is
something that won't change.
It's just now everything is complicated and strange.

Your Children

Feeling helpless is a part of life.
Watching your children struggle, cuts like a knife.

What you wouldn't do to erase their pain, you would
turn back the clock and they would be young again.

Then for them, you could map out a new route,
their life would hold only hope with no doubts.

They would be happy and worry free,
their days would be sunny and carefree.

They will make their way in life of that we are sure.
It's all the things in between we wish they didn't have to endure.

We can only hope our love and guidance will carry them through,
and when life gets tough they get tougher to.

It's what's inside of them that will make them strong,
and if they follow their hearts, they can't go wrong.

56

Your Day

It's your day to treasure memories gone by,
and to look forward to a future only you can create.

It's your day, use your head, but listen
to your heart.

It's your day to celebrate, so take a
deep breath and smile.

It's your day to realize all that life has to offer.

It's your day to be proud of you!

It's your day, a day that paves the way
for your future.

Smile, it's YOUR DAY!

Your Graduation

A great mind should not be wasted.

Use it like a sponge, and soak up
all the knowledge you can.

In every precious life there is a plan.

The world is your map, displayed for
only you to see.

So take that leap of faith, and discover
who you really want to be.

Your Face

Your face is carefully etched in my memory.

Ours was but a short story.

A chance was all I ever wanted.

Instead I'm left lonely and taunted.

You're not what was meant to be.

You left my heart exposed, for everyone to see.

I'll never forget you, or what could've been.

Your memories left echoing in the wind.